THE FOOD INSECURITIES OF ZIMBABWEAN MIGRANTS IN URBAN SOUTH AFRICA

JONATHAN CRUSH AND GODFREY TAWODZERA

SERIES EDITOR: PROF. JONATHAN CRUSH

© AFSUN 2016

Published by the African Food Security Urban Network (AFSUN)
African Centre for Cities, University of Cape Town, Private Bag X3
Rondebosch 7701, South Africa and Balsillie School of International
Affairs, Waterloo, Canada
www.afsun.org

First published 2016

ISBN 978-1-920597-15-3

Cover photo: © Mujahid Safodien/IRIN. Migrants and asylum seekers at
the 'I believe in Jesus Church' shelter for men in the South African border
town of Musina queue up for a free hot meal, provided by the UN's
Refugee Agency (UNHCR)

Production by Bronwen Dachs Muller, Cape Town

Printed by MegaDigital, Cape Town

AUTHORS

Jonathan Crush is CIGI Chair in Global Migration and Development, Balsillie School of International Affairs, Waterloo, Canada, and Honorary Professor at the University of Cape Town.

Godfrey Tawodzera is a Senior Lecturer, Department of Geography and Environmental Sciences, University of Limpopo, Polokwane, South Africa.

Previous Publications in the AFSUN Series

No 1 *The Invisible Crisis: Urban Food Security in Southern Africa*

No 2 *The State of Urban Food Insecurity in Southern Africa*

No 3 *Pathways to Insecurity: Food Supply and Access in Southern African Cities*

No 4 *Urban Food Production and Household Food Security in Southern African Cities*

No 5 *The HIV and Urban Food Security Nexus*

No 6 *Urban Food Insecurity and the Advent of Food Banking in Southern Africa*

No 7 *Rapid Urbanization and the Nutrition Transition in Southern Africa*

No 8 *Climate Change and Food Security in Southern African Cities*

No 9 *Migration, Development and Urban Food Security*

No 10 *Gender and Food Insecurity in Southern African Cities*

No 11 *The State of Urban Food Insecurity in Cape Town*

No 12 *The State of Food Insecurity in Johannesburg*

No 13 *The State of Food Insecurity in Harare, Zimbabwe*

No 14 *The State of Food Insecurity in Windhoek, Namibia*

No 15 *The State of Food Insecurity in Manzini, Swaziland*

No 16 *The State of Food Insecurity in Msunduzi Municipality, South Africa*

No 17 *The State of Food Insecurity in Gaborone, Botswana*

No 18 *The State of Food Insecurity in Blantyre City, Malawi*

No 19 *The State of Food Insecurity in Lusaka, Zambia*

No 20 *The State of Food Insecurity in Maputo, Mozambique*

No 21 *The State of Poverty and Food Insecurity in Maseru, Lesotho*

No 22 *The Return of Food: Poverty and Food Security in Zimbabwe after the Crisis*

CONTENTS

TABLES

FIGURES

1. Introduction

Over the last decade, South Africa has emerged as the major destination for people leaving Zimbabwe.[1] The migration corridor between the two countries is also increasingly well traversed by researchers. In several major volumes of essays and a host of articles, researchers have examined a wide variety of migration themes.[2] These include the dimensions of migration;[3] undocumented migration;[4] the brain drain;[5] diaspora engagement;[6] return migration;[7] abuse of migrants' human rights;[8] migrant identities;[9] the working conditions and livelihood strategies of migrants;[10] and the contradictory and confused policy responses of the South African government to migration from Zimbabwe.[11] Taken as a whole, this rapidly-expanding body of research confirms that migration from Zimbabwe is a complex, dynamic and increasingly diverse phenomenon. However, there are still some notable gaps in our understanding of the drivers and impacts of migration from Zimbabwe. One of the most obvious of these is the relationship between migration and food security. There is a dearth of studies examining the impact of international migration on food security in Zimbabwe and the food security status and challenges faced by migrants living in South Africa.

The general relationship between international migration and food security is not well researched, especially in Africa. This is symptomatic of the wide gulf between these two areas of research and policy making.[12] The migration and development agenda tends to ignore the relationship between international mobility and food security. And much of the discussion on food security focuses on rural populations and livelihoods and downplays the importance of mobility to the survival of urban dwellers. An even more glaring omission is how migrants themselves cope with the challenges of accessing sufficient, good quality food in the cities to which they migrate.

Food insecurity is sometimes seen as one of the root causes of out-migration from the rural areas of the African continent, along with poverty, declining agricultural productivity, and climate change.[13] In addition, food purchase constantly emerges as a major use of remittances in surveys of migrant-sending households. A recent five-country study in Africa by the World Bank found, for example, that the percentage of total remittances spent on food varied from country to country and with whether the source of remittances was within or outside the continent.[14] Senegal had the highest percentages (53% of external and 73% of intra-Africa remittances spent on food) and Uganda the lowest (8% and 10% respectively).[15] An earlier study of five Southern African countries by the Southern African Migration Programme (SAMP) found that 82% of migrant-sending households used remittances to purchase food (the next highest uses, at 52%, were clothing and education).[16] As many as 28% of migrants had also remitted foodstuffs in the previous year (with highs of 60% and 44% respectively in the cases of Mozambican and Zimbabwean migrants).

The relationship between international migration and household food security in sending areas is beginning to command more attention outside Africa, especially in Asia and Latin America.[17] While remittances are widely used by recipient households to purchase food, there have been few attempts to take the analysis further and examine whether remittances have a demonstrable impact on the food security of recipient households and, if so, whether that impact is positive or negative.[18] A recent review of the literature on countries in Africa and the Caribbean concluded that "although there is wealth of research on migrant remittances, none has investigated the relationships between their use at the domestic level and food security."[19] SAMP found that while remittances may have mitigated food insecurity among migrant-sending households in Southern Africa, they certainly did not eliminate it. As many as 47% of the surveyed households reported never having enough food to eat in the previous year, while only 16% said that they always had enough food.[20] A national study in Ghana found that migration did not substantially affect total food expenditures per capita, and had "minimal noticeable effect on food expenditure patterns."[21] In high migration regions, however, out-migration increased overall food expenditures resulting in a shift towards the consumption of potentially less nutritious categories of food.

Studies of the changing health status of international migrants at their destination are more common, especially in relation to the changing food consumption practices and diets of migrants and immigrants in North America and Europe. This research literature is framed by two ideas. First, there is what is known as the "healthy immigrant effect."[22] The argument here is that recent migrants tend to be healthier across a range of indicators than those they have left behind, than long-term immigrants, and than local populations. Three explanations have been advanced for the effect: health screening policies by destination country authorities prior to migration; favourable habits and behaviours of individuals in the origin country prior to migration; and immigrant self-selection whereby the healthiest and wealthiest source country residents are most likely to have the financial and physical means to migrate.[23] However, while these explanations might apply to skilled immigrants who enter countries such as Canada, the UK and Australia, it does not address the situation with other kinds of movement, such as lower-skilled temporary migration. As a result, there is no solid evidence on whether the "effect" applies to the growing numbers of temporary migrants in the North and the South. However, various studies of resettled African refugee groups have suggested that refugees experience higher levels of food insecurity and poorer diets than host populations.[24]

There is considerable evidence that the quality of diets of immigrants in Europe and North America declines over time and comes to approximate that of the local population. This empirical observation has given rise to the second main hypothesis – the "acculturation thesis."[25] The argument here is that there are culturally-driven forces that encourage or force migrants to eat unhealthy, processed foods that are the staple of the native-born in these countries. One of the major documented consequences is a growth over time in overnutrition or obesity among immigrant populations.[26] Once again, the thesis has been applied mostly to long-term immigrant residents of destination countries in Europe and North America, and not temporary migrants in the North or South.[27] Studies of the changing diets of African immigrants in Europe and North America have also been influenced by these two ideas.[28]

Both the healthy immigrant and acculturation arguments have been developed and tested almost exclusively in the context of migration from South to North and permanent settlement in the North. Neither has been applied in any systematic way to migration within the South itself (or so-called South-South migration). Key questions that need research include the following: What strategies do migrants adopt in countries of destination to earn income and what proportion of their income is spent on food? Do migrants experience greater food insecurity than the local population in each of the various standard categories of food security – food availability, food accessibility, food quality, and food regularity? Are migrants more or less vulnerable to undernutrition and overnutrition than non-migrants? Does the quality of their diet change after migration? Where do migrants tend to source their foods, what foods do they consume and with what consequences for their well-being?

This report focuses on people involved in South-South migration, in this case Zimbabweans in South African urban areas. It therefore addresses a major neglected topic in the emerging literature on migration and food security. This study of Zimbabwean migrants in South Africa set out to answer the general questions outlined above as well as some more specific issues including: What are the levels of household food insecurity among migrants in general and Zimbabwean migrants in particular in South African cities? What are the major causes of household food insecurity? What are the general experiences of food insecurity among different types of migrant household? And what responses and strategies are adopted to deal with food insecurity within the household?

2. MIGRATION FROM ZIMBABWE TO SOUTH AFRICA

"Mixed migration" from Zimbabwe to South Africa since the end of apartheid has become more heterogeneous over time.[29] The overall number of migrants has been a source of considerable speculation and exaggeration by the South African media and government officials. Certainly, the amount of cross-border traffic between the two countries has increased considerably from less than 200,000 in the mid-1980s to around 600,000 in 2004 to over 1.6 million in 2010 (Figure 1). However, a considerable proportion are temporary visitors, visiting South Africa to trade, to visit family or to seek medical attention. Using various projections, the number of black Zimbabweans in South Africa was estimated at 509,000 in 2007.[30] The 2011 South African Census recorded a total of 515,824 Zimbabweans in South Africa aged 15-64. This should not be interpreted as a stabilization of migration from Zimbabwe after 2007 (since the latter figure excludes children) although it is likely that migration has slowed after political and economic stability was partially restored in Zimbabwe in 2009-2010.

FIGURE 1: Legal Entries from Zimbabwe to South Africa, 1983-2010

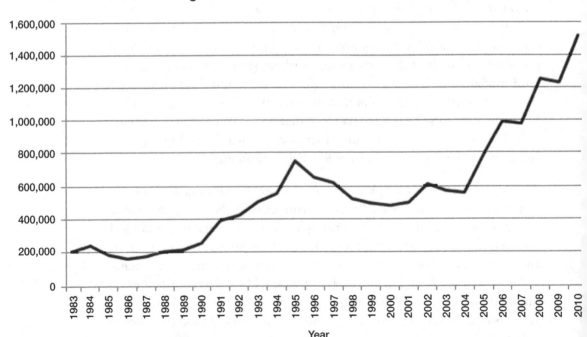

Source: Statistics South Africa

For most of the 1990s, the defining characteristic of migration from Zimbabwe to South Africa was its temporary oscillating character. Most migrants returned home frequently and showed very little inclination to remain in South Africa for more than a short time. In a SAMP survey of Zimbabwean migrants in 2005, nearly one-third of migrants said they returned to Zimbabwe at least once a month and 50% of migrants returned at least once every few months.[31] However, there is growing evidence that over the last decade, migration to South Africa has taken on a more permanent character, despite the best efforts of the South African government to prevent this. A SAMP survey in 2010 focused on migrants who had come to South Africa for the first time after 2005, and found that less than 1% returned to Zimbabwe once a month and only 9% returned once every few months (Table 1).[32] As many as 46% had not been back to Zimbabwe since coming to South Africa and just as many said that they wanted to remain in South Africa "for a few years." Another 13% said they wished to remain "indefinitely" and another 8% "permanently." In other words, two-thirds of the migrants viewed a long-term stay in South Africa as desirable.

Table 1: Frequency of Return to Zimbabwe		
	2005 (%)	2010 (%)
At least once per month	31	<1
Once every few months	19	9
Once or twice per year	26	28
Other	25	9
Not returned	0	46
Cannot return	0	3
Will never return	0	2

The socio-economic and demographic profile of the Zimbabwean migrant population in South Africa underwent several changes as out-migration became a more widespread response to the political and economic crisis in Zimbabwe.[33] The proportion of female migrants was already high by regional standards in the late 1990s, but increased still further in the years that followed (Table 2). The proportion of migrants under the age of 25 also increased over time, even as the proportion over 40 years old dwindled. Over half of migrants at all times were in their late twenties and thirties. Consistent with this pattern, the proportion of unmarried migrants grew, almost doubling between 1997 and 2010, while the proportion of married migrants fell by 25%. The proportion of household heads in the migrant population did not vary as much, but the numbers of adult sons and daughters did (increasing from 20% in 1997 to 50% in 2005).

Table 2: Demographic Profile of Zimbabwean Migrants, 1997-2010			
	1997	2005	2010
Sex (%)			
Male	61	56	56
Female	39	44	44
Age (%)			
15–24	26	15	31
25–39 (25-44)	(50)	56	59
>40 (>45)	(23)	24	10
Marital status (%)			
Married	66	58	41
Formerly married	8	11	10
Unmarried	25	31	49
Status in household (%)			
Household head	34	28	28
Spouse	26	13	15
Sons/daughters	20	50	43
Other family	7	9	12
Other	13	1	2
Source: SAMP			

3. RESEARCH METHODOLOGY

Although Zimbabwean migrants live in many of South Africa's urban areas, this study was conducted in the main destinations of Cape Town and Johannesburg. These cities are the largest in South Africa and constitute major centres for livelihood and employment opportunity among Zimbabwean migrants.[34] In each city, the study identified three residential areas known to be inhabited by large numbers of Zimbabweans. In Cape Town, Du Noon, Masiphumelele, and Nyanga were selected while in Johannesburg, Orange Farm, Johannesburg Central, and Alexandra Park were chosen (Table 3). All are low-income areas but represent different kinds of neighbourhoods: informal settlements (Orange Farm and Du Noon), inner city areas (Johannesburg Central), and townships (Alexandra Park, Masiphumelele and Nyanga). It is therefore important to emphasize that this is not a study of the food security of the Zimbabwean migrant population as a whole, but rather of poorer, less-skilled migrants.

The research focused on the household rather than the individual migrant. However, data on 762 individual household members was collected in the survey of 500 households. In the absence of a reliable sampling frame, and because most migrants have self-settled among the local population, the survey employed snowball sampling to identify respondents. This involved identifying a small number of initial respondents and using them to identify subsequent interviewees through their own networks. Eighteen Zimbabwean field researchers were recruited and trained to collect data in both cities. The survey was done in November and December 2011.

TABLE 3: Survey Areas			
Survey area	No. of households	% of city sample	% of total sample
Cape Town			
Masiphumelele	63	25.2	12.6
Nyanga	93	37.2	18.6
Du Noon	94	37.6	18.8
Sub-totals	250		50.0
Johannesburg			
Central	101	40.4	20.2
Alexandra Park	69	27.6	13.8
Orange Farm	80	32.0	16.0
Sub-totals	150		50.0
Total	500		100.0

The qualitative component of the research involved 50 in-depth interviews with selected household heads and 10 focus group discussions. These sought to elicit detailed food security experiences as well as understand how poor migrant households cope in a foreign land. Combined, the in-depth interviews, focus group discussions and survey sought to capture information and experiences about food security status, dietary quality, household food sources, alternative livelihood strategies, as well as other relevant food security data.

4. MIGRANT HOUSEHOLD COMPOSITION

In most poor areas of Southern African cities, male-centred households (that is, households with a male head and no partner or spouse) are in the minority. Of the 6,452 households in 11 cities surveyed by AFSUN in 2007-2008, for example, only 12% were male-centred (Table 4). Female-centred households were far more numerous (at 34%), followed by nuclear households (32%) and extended family households (22%). Over one-third of the sample (38%) were migrant households (in which every household member was born outside the city). The profile of migrant households was quite different: the proportion of male-centred households was significantly higher (at 23%) and the proportion of extended family households much lower (at 12%).

Among the Zimbabwean migrant households in the current survey, the proportion of male-centred households was even higher (at 39%) and the proportion of extended family households lower at only 10%. The fact that male-centred households are in the majority (three times as common as in the AFSUN sample as a whole) suggests that male migration still dominates the migration corridor between Zimbabwe and South Africa. However, just because male migrants establish their own households in South Africa (or live alone), it does not necessarily follow that they are unattached since many married migrants choose to leave their partners and children in Zimbabwe. Nearly one-third of the respondent households were female-centred, confirming that migration streams from Zimbabwe comprise a significant number of independent female migrants.[35] Migration from Zimbabwe to South Africa is far more feminized than it is from other countries in the region.[36] SAMP surveys of Zimbabwean migrants in 2005 and 2010, for example, found that women constituted about 44% of post-2005 migrants.[37]

TABLE 4: Household Structure			
	% all AFSUN households	% migrant AFSUN households	% Zimbabwean migrant households
Female-centred	34	37	30
Male-centred	12	23	39
Nuclear	32	28	20
Extended	22	12	10
N	6,536	2,053	497

Household size was small with an average of less than two. In part, this was because almost two-thirds of the households were single-person units and another 23% were two-person households. Only 10% of the households had three persons and 2% four persons. In the entire sample, there were only three five-person households (the largest household size). That said, migration from Zimbabwe has increasingly involved settlement of nuclear families in South Africa. Usually the head of household moves first and is joined by dependants. Indicative of the growth of family migration, 15% of the household members in this survey were under the age of 20 and 8% were children under 10 (Figure 2). However, the small number of extended families suggests that elderly dependants are not moving to South Africa and also that households may be unwilling to take in extended family members while they themselves are struggling. The members of the surveyed households were all relatively young, with 44% in their twenties and 31% in their thirties. Only 1% were over 50 years old.

FIGURE 2: Age of Zimbabwean Migrants

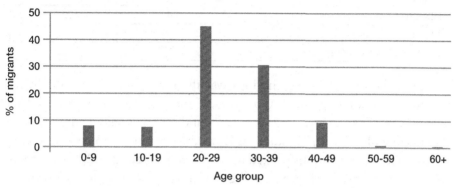

5. REASONS FOR MIGRATION

The reasons given by respondents for migrating were dominated by a comparison of living conditions in the two countries. As many as 84% of the respondents mentioned this as a reason for moving (Table 5). Three-quarters also said they had moved in order to work in the informal sector, an expression of the difficulty of obtaining jobs in the formal economy. Only 30% said they had moved to South Africa to work in the formal sector. A sizeable percentage (44%) reported moving because of food shortages and hunger in Zimbabwe. In an environment characterized by high unemployment, a contracting economy and hyperinflation, hunger and food shortages were an everyday occurrence after 2005.[38] An AFSUN survey in Harare in 2008, for example, recorded extremely high levels of food insecurity among poor households in the city.[39]

Table 5: Reasons for Migration to South Africa		
	No.	% of households
Overall living conditions	420	84.0
Informal sector job	356	71.2
Food/hunger	222	44.4
Formal sector job	151	30.2
Moved with family	82	16.4
Education/schools	66	13.2
Safety of self/family	75	15.0
Attractions of urban life	31	6.2
Asylum	31	6.2
Marriage	28	5.6
Political exile	23	4.6
Drought	21	4.2
Freedom/democracy/peace	13	2.6

Sent to live with family	7	1.4
Death	4	0.5
Housing	2	0.3
Note: multiple response question		

One of the more striking findings was the low rating given to political motivations for migration. Only 6% of the respondents said they had moved to South Africa to seek asylum and 5% that they had gone into political exile. An earlier study of Zimbabweans in Johannesburg found that political motivations peaked in the years from 2002 to 2004 and then declined sharply.[40] However, refugee claims by Zimbabwean migrants soared in the period after 2004, peaking at over 140,000 in 2009 (Figure 3). What this indicates is that many migrants were using the asylum-seeker process to legitimize their presence in South Africa and avoid deportation. Recognizing this fact, the South African government offered an amnesty to Zimbabweans in 2010 (extended in 2014 for a further three years), which incentivized 250,000 migrants to relinquish their claims for asylum in exchange for temporary residence and work permits.[41]

FIGURE 3: Applications for Asylum by Zimbabweans in South Africa, 2000-2010

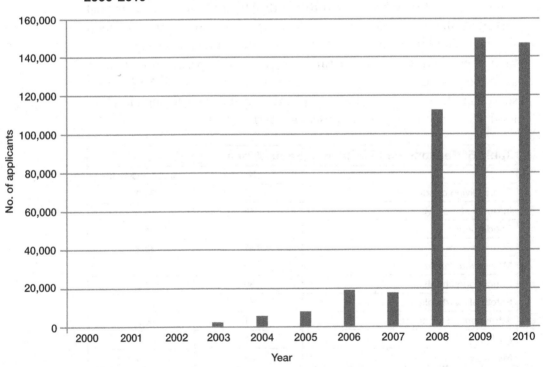

Because there is evidence of growing onward migration from Johannesburg and Cape Town, the respondents were asked if they had considered moving elsewhere. As many as 63% responded in the affirmative (Table 6). Of these, almost half indicated that their preferred destination was a different South African city. Just over a quarter of those thinking about onward migration were interested in international migration to Europe and North America and 18% to another African country (Botswana being the most likely destination). A significant proportion of the respondents (61%) said they were likely to be better off in a different city or country.

TABLE 6: Preferred Destinations for Onward Migration

Preferred destination	Johannesburg		Cape Town		Total	
	No.	%	No.	%	No.	%
Another South African city	83	53.5	71	44.7	154	49.0
International (non-African) destination	42	27.2	44	27.7	86	27.4
Other African country	21	13.5	36	22.6	57	18.1
South African rural area	9	5.8	8	5.0	17	3.4
Total	155	100.0	159	100.0	314	100.0

The vast majority of respondents (80%) considered migration to South Africa to be important for the survival of the members of the household. A mere 5% rated it as unimportant. Two-thirds (65%) also said that the effect of migration on the household was positive or very positive, while 16% said that it had been negative or very negative. In the qualitative interviews and focus groups, many argued that despite difficulties in finding employment and low remuneration in South Africa, their socio-economic conditions were considerably better than they had been in Zimbabwe. Those who reported a neutral impact (around 17%) mostly argued that they were still looking for employment.

Some migrants indicated that unemployment levels in Cape Town and Johannesburg were making it difficult for them to secure jobs there and that their chances of finding work in other centres might be better. In addition, most of the employed were in a precarious position with temporary jobs. Some were underpaid by unscrupulous employers, aware that they had little recourse to the law. Others said that competition in the labour market with the large numbers of Zimbabwean migrants in Johannesburg and Cape Town drove down wages.

6. EDUCATION AND EMPLOYMENT PROFILE

Access to wage employment is critical to migrants in urban areas primarily because it is the major source of household income. However, this particular migrant cohort was reasonably well-educated. Just 5% of the total household adult population had a primary education or less, 21% had some secondary education and 56% had completed high school (Table 7). A smaller number (16%) had post-secondary qualifications. In other words, the majority of these migrants were only in a position to access unskilled and semi-skilled tiers of the South African labour market.

TABLE 7: Highest Level of Education of Adult Household Members		
	No.	%
No formal schooling	3	0.5
Some primary	11	1.7
Primary completed	18	2.8
Some high school	138	21.5
High school completed	359	55.8
Post-secondary qualifications not university	90	14.0
Some university	12	1.9
University completed	2	0.3
Post graduate	10	1.6
Total	643	100.0

About half of the members of the sampled households were employed, with 31% working full-time and 19% part-time. This was a 12% drop from the SAMP survey results in 2010, which found that 62% of Zimbabwean migrants in these two cities were in full or part-time employment.[42] Such a decrease is probably a result of the increasing difficulty of finding employment, especially when Zimbabwean migrants have to compete with South Africans and other migrants for scarce jobs. Nearly 40% of household heads (and 36% of all household members) were working informally (Table 8). In both cities, migrants were selling sweets, crafts, compact discs, and other paraphernalia at major train stations, bus stations and along main roads in the areas in which they lived. Some also worked as producers, primarily of handicrafts, and as advertisers for other informal vendors (such as sangomas). A total of 15% of the migrants were in unskilled manual work.

The three most common employment sectors were services (11% of household heads and 10% of all migrants), domestic work (9% and 11%)

and security (5% and 4%). Most of those in the service industry were employed in hotels, restaurants and bars as waiters, bartenders and general hands. Domestic workers were almost exclusively female. High-skilled jobs were held by 13% of household heads and 12% of all migrants. Occupations in this category included professionals, teachers, office workers and skilled manual workers. However, some of the jobs that migrants were doing were unrelated to their areas of professional training, with teachers, nurses, and other professional workers being employed as domestic workers and general hands. During interviews and focus group discussions, migrants indicated that living in a foreign land where jobs were scarce meant that they did not have the luxury of choice and took on any kind of employment to earn a living. While most skilled migrants accept lower-skilled jobs as a stopgap measure and hope to secure employment in their field of training later, this often proves difficult.

TABLE 8: Main Occupation of Household Head and Household Members				
	Household heads		Household members	
	No.	%	No.	%
Skilled	52	13.1	67	12.4
Skilled manual worker	14	3.5	19	3.5
Business (self-employed)	12	3.0	13	2.4
Office worker	9	1.7	15	2.8
Professional worker	9	1.7	11	2.0
Teacher	5	1.0	6	1.1
Employer/manager	3	0.6	3	0.5
Semi-skilled	114	28.7	161	29.8
Service worker	43	10.8	63	11.7
Domestic worker	36	9.1	61	11.3
Security personnel	20	5.0	21	3.9
Truck driver	9	2.3	9	1.7
Mineworker	3	0.8	3	0.6
Police/military	2	0.5	2	0.4
Foreman	1	0.2	2	0.4
Low skilled	218	54.9	275	50.9
Informal economy	155	39.0	192	35.6
Unskilled manual worker	63	15.9	83	15.4
Other	15	3.8	3	0.6
Total	397	100.0	540	100.0

Survival in the challenging South African urban environment demands that household members engage in other activities to augment income from formal employment. As Figure 4 shows, the most common additional household livelihood strategy was casual labour with 45% of households reporting this as a strategy. Casual employment included work such as gardening, washing clothes, handing out advertising leaflets at traffic lights and washing cars. Just over one-quarter (27%) of households had members involved in the marketing of various goods at major transport terminals, on the streets, and door-to-door. It is certainly not uncommon to find household members employed as teachers or office workers during the week and peddling their wares on weekends. Other strategies included selling handmade items such as baskets, wire and metal toys, brooms, wood and stone carvings, and crotcheted items.

FIGURE 4: Alternative Household Livelihood Strategies

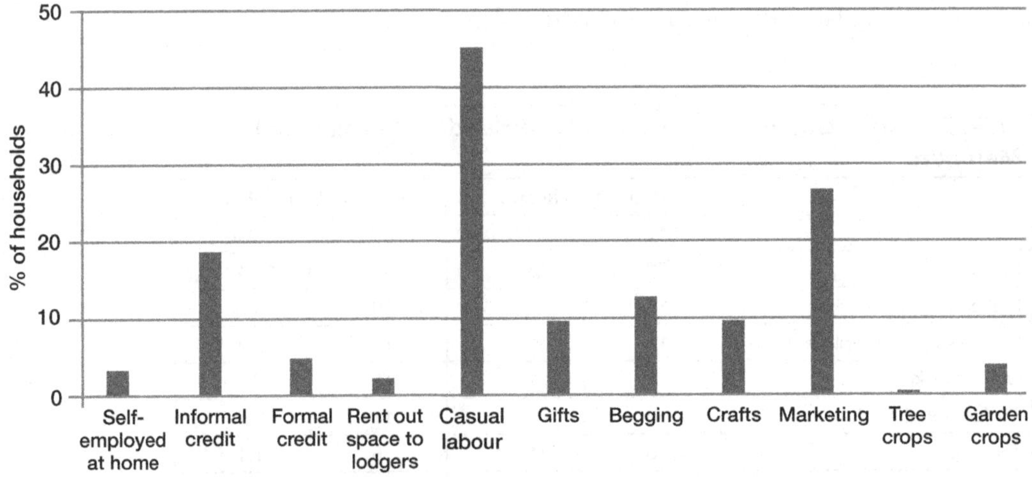

Credit – both informal and formal – was being utilized as an additional livelihood strategy. Informal credit involves borrowing from fellow Zimbabweans and from local loan sharks at high rates of interest. Respondents indicated that most loan sharks were averse to lending to international migrants because of the risk that they would return to their home country without settling their debts. Migrants who took out loans were therefore required to deposit some form of security, such as cellphones, beds, television sets, sewing machines and computers, which could be sold should the borrower abscond or be unable to repay. Some complained that they had lost valuable goods as collateral for debts that were considerably lower than the value of the assets deposited. Those who had lost assets said that they were aware of the risks, but were pushed by poverty and desperation to make the transaction. Households having difficulties finding casual work or other forms of income often resorted to begging. Most were women and children who beg in the streets or go from door to door begging for money or food.

7. HOUSEHOLD INCOME AND LEVELS OF POVERTY

Despite household heads saying they were better off after moving from Zimbabwe, many were struggling to get by. The mean monthly income of the households in the survey was extremely low at only ZAR1,433 per month, with a minimum of ZAR100 and a maximum of ZAR8,500. As Figure 5 indicates, 17% of the households reported a monthly income of ZAR500 or less, while 32% reported incomes between ZAR501 and ZAR1,000. In other words, about half of the households had incomes of ZAR1,000 or less per month, hardly adequate for the many urban expenses that need to be met. Only 2% of the households reported incomes of over ZAR4,000 per month.

FIGURE 5: Household Average Monthly Income

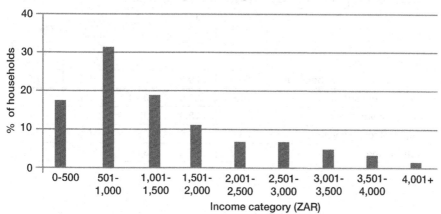

In addition to the income poverty suggested by these figures, the Afrobarometer's Lived Poverty Index (LPI) was used to measure the subjective experience of poverty.[43] The LPI scores range from 0.00 (complete satisfaction of basic needs) to 4.00 (frequent shortages of basic needs). The average LPI for the sample households was 2.06, with a minimum of 0.80 and a maximum of 4.00 (Table 9). This was significantly higher than the 0.60 LPI recorded for Johannesburg or the 1.01 recorded in Cape Town in the 2008 AFSUN surveys. This indicates higher levels of lived poverty among the migrant population. More than half of the surveyed households had an LPI in the 2.01-3.00 category while only 2% had an LPI of between 0.00 and 1.00.

Such high levels of lived poverty certainly reflect low absolute incomes, the costs of surviving in a large city, and the inaccessibility of formal safety nets such as child grants. As many as 46% of the households said that they had frequently gone without a cash income in the year prior to the survey (Table 10). In addition, 92% of the households reported that they had gone without food to eat, while between 70-80% had gone without other basic necessities such as clean water, medicine or medical treatment, electricity and cooking oil.

TABLE 9: Lived Poverty Index (LPI) Categories

Lived Poverty Index (LPI) categories	Johannes-burg		Cape Town		Total	
	No.	%	No.	%	No.	%
0.00-1.00 Never to seldom without	6	2.4	5	2.0	11	2.2
1.01-2.00 Seldom to sometimes without	96	38.4	85	34.0	181	36.2
2.01-3.00 Sometimes to often without	141	56.4	151	60.4	292	58.4
3.01-4.00 Often to always without	7	2.8	9	3.6	16	3.2

TABLE 10: Frequency of Going Without Basic Needs

	Never	Just once or twice	Several times	Many times	Always
Enough food to eat	7.8	41.4	39.0	10.2	1.6
Enough clean water for home use	25.0	29.6	31.4	6.2	7.6
Medicine or medical treatment	21.4	31.0	34.0	12.2	1.0
Electricity in your home	23.8	28.8	38.0	6.6	2.6
Enough fuel to cook your food	29.8	25.6	35.6	5.2	3.6
A cash income	2.2	17.6	34.6	24.4	21.2

8. LEVELS OF MIGRANT FOOD INSECURITY

The survey instrument used in this study was the standard AFSUN urban food security baseline survey. AFSUN uses four international cross-cultural scales developed by the Food and Nutrition Technical Assistance (FANTA) project to assess levels of food insecurity:

- Household Food Insecurity Access Scale (HFIAS): The HFIAS measures the degree of food insecurity during the month prior to the survey.[44] An HFIAS score is calculated for each household based on answers to nine "frequency-of-occurrence" questions. The minimum score is 0 and the maximum is 27. The higher the score, the more food insecurity the household experienced.

- Household Food Insecurity Access Prevalence Indicator (HFIAP): The HFIAP indicator uses the responses to the HFIAS questions to group all households into four food security categories: food secure, mildly food insecure, moderately food insecure and severely food insecure.[45]

- Household Dietary Diversity Scale (HDDS): Dietary diversity refers to how many food groups were consumed within the household in the previous 24 hours.[46] The maximum number, based on the FAO classification of food groups for Africa, is 12. An increase in the average number of different food groups consumed provides a quantifiable measure of improved household access to a varied diet.

- Months of Adequate Household Food Provisioning Indicator (MAHFP): The MAHFP indicator captures changes in the household's ability to ensure that food is available year round.[47] Households are asked to identify in which months (during the past 12) they did not have access to sufficient food to meet their household needs.

The average household HFIAS score of the Zimbabwean migrant households was 14.39, with a median of 14.00, a minimum of 0 and a maximum of 27. This score was considerably higher than the 10.7 recorded for Cape Town in the 2008 AFSUN survey or the 4.7 recorded for Johannesburg. This finding suggests that migrants are a great deal more vulnerable to food insecurity than their local counterparts in the poorer areas of these cities. On the HFIAP scale, 11% of households fell into the food secure category while another 5% were classified as mildly food insecure (Table 11). The majority of migrant households were either moderately food insecure (24%) or severely food insecure (60%). Levels of food insecurity among Zimbabwean migrants in Cape Town and Johannesburg were lower than those in Harare, Zimbabwe, which is consistent with the finding that hunger and food insecurity are important drivers of migration. While not all of the migrants in South Africa were from Harare, the comparison is still instructive and suggests that migration improved the food security situation of migrant households. Whether it brought them up to the level of all households in the cities of destination is another matter.

TABLE 11: Household Food Security Status				
	Zimbabwe migrant households (%)	Harare households (%)	Cape Town households (%)	Johannesburg households (%)
Food secure	11	2	15	44
Mildly food insecure	5	3	5	14
Moderately food insecure	24	24	12	15
Severely food insecure	60	72	68	27

The AFSUN survey found marked differences in levels of food insecurity between poor neighbourhoods in Cape Town and Johannesburg.[48] In Cape Town, only 20% of households were food secure or mildly food insecure while in Johannesburg, the figure was 58%. Or again, 68% of Cape Town households were severely food insecure compared to only 27% of Johannesburg households. The levels of food insecurity of all poor Cape Town households and Zimbabwean migrant households in both cities are relatively similar. In the case of Johannesburg, on the other hand, there are significant differences (44% versus 11% food secure and 27% versus 60% severely food insecure). The particular difficulties of survival in Johannesburg were captured in the in-depth interviews and focus groups. As one respondent noted:

> Life is really difficult. The food is never enough and I have gone hungry many times. It is particularly bad on weekends when kitchen soup houses are closed. Yes, things were really terrible in Zimbabwe and that made us come here, but to be honest, I am still struggling. I have to survive on charity and begging. It is tough, as I am not working.[49]

Many indicated that the situation was so bad that they could only afford to eat a single meal a day. The severity of household food insecurity for the migrant households was reflected not only in the high prevalence of food insecurity, but also in the narrow range of foods that were being consumed. According to one respondent:

> It is difficult to afford the food we want. We eat the same kind of food day in and day out. Usually we eat *pap* and *maguru/matumbu* (offal) because that is what is cheap. With *matumbu* at least you can budget your little money. But we also need to eat beef, but it is expensive. I do not know when I last ate beef…maybe over a year ago, I don't know. It's the same food over and over again. There is no variety, but there is nothing that we can do. I guess we have to be grateful that at least we can get a meal here and there.[50]

Another indicated that they concentrated on starchy foods, as they were cheaper and lasted longer:

> We also want to eat these nice foods, but we cannot afford them. It is pointless trying to buy good food and then eat for one week and then struggle for the rest of the month. So we would rather buy the ordinary stuff that stays longer. We therefore buy mealie-meal, cooking oil, salt, and sugar for these are the basic foodstuffs that we consume in this house. That way we can keep our stomachs full.[51]

The Household Dietary Diversity Scale results validate such assertions and indicate that a lack of dietary diversity is typical of a large number of migrant households. The mean HDDS was only 5.08 out of a possible score of 12.00, indicating that households had, on average, consumed foods from only five different food groups in the previous 24 hours. Nearly half of the households (46%) had HDDS scores of 4 or lower (Figure 6).

FIGURE 6: Household Dietary Diversity Score

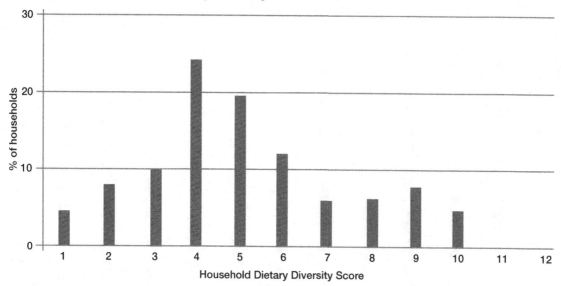

Foods consumed by most households included cereals and other foods made from grain, primarily maize, (93%); meat, poultry or offal (59%); sugar or honey (55%); other foods such as tea and coffee (50%) and foods made with oils, butter or fat (49%) (Figure 7). What is important to note is that the bulk of the food being consumed by households is high in starch and with high concentrations of sugar and oils. Protein and vitamin-rich foods were consumed in only a minority of households.

Besides household food security and dietary diversity, the survey also investigated the number of months in the previous year that households were adequately provisioned. Only 10% of the households in the sample did not experience any months of inadequate food provisioning. The average number of months of adequate household food provisioning was only 7.2. Thus, on average, households experienced food shortages for about 4.8 months per year, a clear indication of the depth of food insecurity. The months of greatest inadequacy were from January to March and again in September and October (Figure 8).

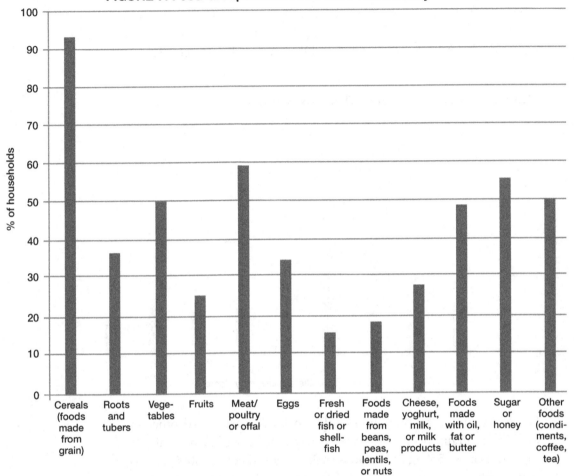

FIGURE 7: Food Groups Consumed the Previous Day

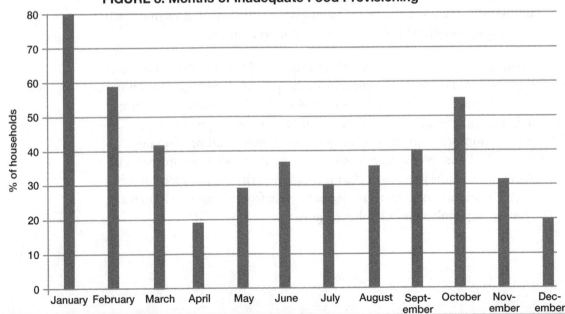

FIGURE 8: Months of Inadequate Food Provisioning

Eighty percent of the households reported inadequate food provision in January, falling to 59% in February and 41% in March. Migrants indicated that the primary reason that these are the lean months of the year is excessive spending during the festive season, which exhausts their meagre savings. During these months they are therefore working to pay off debts acquired during the festivities. Other migrants indicated that they usually travel to Zimbabwe for the festive season. Because many are in temporary employment, they return in January to look for new jobs and, in some cases, remain unemployed for a while at the beginning of the year. Some companies close in December and only open again in February, further depriving employees of badly needed income at the start of the year. Between September and December, most migrant households save to cover the expenses that they will incur during the festivities as well as travelling costs. As one respondent explained:

> Right now (November) we are saving money that we will use next month. In fact, I started saving last month. You see, one needs a lot of money to go home to Zimbabwe. I stay in Kariba, over 300 kilometres from Harare, so I need bus fare to take me to Harare, then onwards to Kariba. That is more than R2,000 of bus fare from here. Because I will be travelling in December, transport charges will also be high, so I will need more money and also to pay to transport my luggage, which may be more expensive than the fare for the person. My family back home will be expecting a lot of goods because I have not been home for the whole of this year. So that is a lot of money needed. I also have to pay rent for the month of December even though I will not be here, because if I do not do that, then I will have a problem on return. For me, these two months of October and November are very difficult months for I have to save. Otherwise I may not be able to go home.[52]

Preparation for travel home, and the journey itself, requires funds that reduce the resources available to migrant households to buy food. Some respondents indicated that they eat the bare minimum during these months so that they are able to save for the journey and take care of their families when they go back home.

9. FOOD SOURCES AND COPING STRATEGIES

The spatial distribution of food retail outlets is a significant determinant of vulnerability for poor urban consumers. This is because intra-urban food distribution networks are tilted in favour of high-income residential areas and because high-income earners usually have the flexibility of private transportation.[53] In higher-income areas, infrastructure such as roads, retail and marketing systems is usually well-established and functional. In contrast, network systems in low-income areas of the city are generally poor. This creates disparities in the pricing system as food reaches low-income areas through informal rather than formal supply chains. Despite this observation, the supermarket turns out to be the most significant food source for Zimbabwean migrants in Cape Town and Johannesburg. A total of 96% of the sampled households indicated that they shopped at supermarkets and 21% did so on a daily basis (Table 12). Patronage of the informal food economy was also significant, with 93% of respondents regularly buying food from informal vendors and 38% doing so every day. Small retail outlets and fast food outlets were the third most important source, at 87% and 21% respectively.

TABLE 12: Household Food Sources		
	% of households using source	% of households using source on daily basis
Supermarket	96	21
Informal market/street food	93	38
Small shop/restaurant/take away	87	21
Borrow from others	33	3
Share meals with neighbours and/or friends	29	5
Food provided by neighbours and/or other households	24	4
Food aid	9	8
Community food kitchen	6	1
Remittances (food)	6	1
Grow it	1	0

Hardly any of the migrant households were engaged in urban agriculture. However, they did have higher rates of food sharing than poor households in general. For example, 33% of the migrant households regularly borrow food from one another, 29% share meals with neighbours and friends, and 24% consume food provided by other households. During the in-depth interviews, respondents indicated that redistribution of food was one of the main ways to weather difficult periods as lending, borrowing and sharing helped to spread the risk and avert the total collapse of households. As one observed:

> We are a community of sharing. If you are unable to help others when they are in dire need, they will also not help you when you are in trouble. Our communities and networks have memories – very long memories and we know who gives and who doesn't. Especially as we

are far away from home, we have learnt to support each other. If I have some food, then my neighbours will not starve.[54]

Although the surveyed households were generally poor and food-deprived, they still shared food among themselves, suggesting a greater degree of community solidarity and positive social capital than among the poor urban population in general.[55]

Nearly one-quarter of the households were receiving aid in the form of cash, food or other in-kind contributions. Seventeen percent were receiving assistance from faith-based organizations, 10% from community-based organizations (CBOs) and 5% from non-governmental organizations (NGOs). In Johannesburg, most of the households receiving aid were living in the CBD where they were being sheltered and given food by various churches and NGOs operating in the area.[56] Some churches offered food on Mondays, Wednesdays and Fridays, while others did so on Tuesdays and Thursdays. Few provided assistance on weekends and many migrants indicated that without the help of soup kitchens, the weekends were very difficult for them. In Cape Town, migrants in Du Noon and Masiphumelele also indicated that they had access to food from faith-based organizations and NGOs. Some even boarded trains to the CBD to access food from food aid centres. Two soup kitchens in Cape Town were observed selling food to the poor for 5c a plate.

During a focus group discussion in Central Johannesburg, migrants took turns to explain the importance of the aid that they were getting from faith-based organizations, indicating that without this support, they would have left the country, died or be in prison for having committed crimes in order to feed themselves:

> This church has been good to us. Were it not for them, some of us would have long perished. I can tell you that I have been staying here for the past two years and I have seen others come and go. But one thing that we all agree on is that we are very lucky to have been accommodated here. Even though now they give us just one meal per week, we are within walking distance of two soup kitchens and we get food from there. The food is not much, but it is what makes us survive.[57]

In Cape Town also, migrants reported that they were fed by church-based organizations and relied heavily on this help. In addition to food aid, migrants rely on a variety of other coping strategies when food is short (Figure 9). These include reliance on less expensive foodstuffs (84% of households), poorer quality food (78%) and less preferred but cheaper foods (74%). Over half said that they reduced the number of meals eaten per day, borrowed money to buy food, or solicited the help of a friend or relative. Nearly 50% said that they reduced portion sizes while 20% responded by buying food on credit and reducing the amount of food consumed by adults in the household.

FIGURE 9: Dietary Strategies Used by Households during Shortages

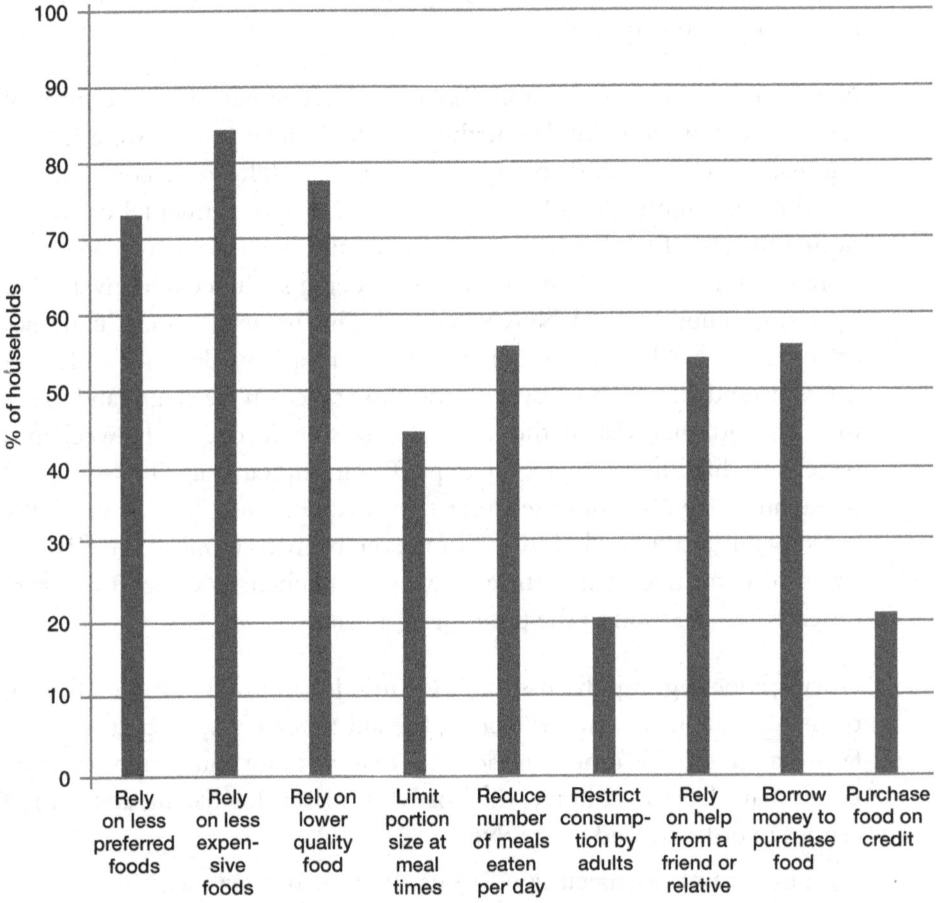

In the in-depth interviews and focus groups, migrants indicated that when the situation is tough, they do not pay much attention to the quality of the food that they are buying. Instead they are preoccupied with simply getting enough food for the household to survive. One respondent in Cape Town explained the trade-offs between the quality and quantity of food as follows:

> We know a lot about food quality and the desirability for us to have such good food. That we know. Our only problem as a household is that we do not have the money to buy such foods. So, when I go to the market or shops, I make sure that what I buy is enough for a long time, be it a week or two weeks. I now know where the bargains are. In some of the shops they sell food that is about to expire and if we are lucky we get some before other people grab the lot. When I go to the

vegetable market I get a lot of food by buying the breakages – tomatoes that have been squashed, onions that are dirty, carrots that are damaged, and so on. These are cheap so I get more. A hard time teaches you how to survive and I can say I have been taught by experience.[58]

Because households purchase the bulk of their food, adjustments are also made to the household budget as a way of coping with food shortages. These strategies include diverting money from paying bills, rent and utilities to purchase food (23%), using long-term savings (35%), and changing place of residence (23%) (Figure 10). While not paying bills can bring eviction notices, migrants pointed out that there are times when there was no option but to abscond, buy food and face the consequences later. An increasing number of migrants were combining households to reduce housing expenses and save money for food and other purchases.

FIGURE 10: Household Coping Strategies

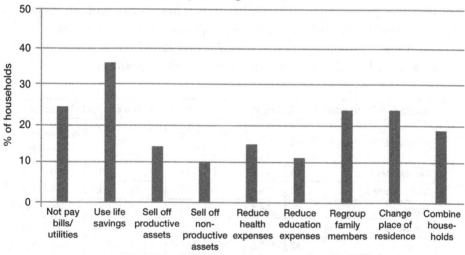

10. DETERMINANTS OF MIGRANT HOUSEHOLD FOOD INSECURITY

In the sampled population as a whole, nuclear households made up the greatest proportion of the food secure (at 35% of the total), followed by male-centred households (28%), extended households (19%) and female-centred households (17%) (Table 13). At the other end of the spectrum, male-centred households comprised 45% of the severely food insecure, followed by female-centred households (33%), nuclear households (15%) and extended households (6%). Thus, households with a head and partner would appear to be more food secure than those with a single head.

However, these figures are partially a function of the different sample sizes of the different types of households, so it is important to examine also the distribution of households within each group. This certainly confirms that food security varies by household type.

Levels of food security were lowest among female-centred and male-centred households (7% and 8%) (Table 14). Similarly, these two types had the highest proportions of severely food insecure households (66% and 69%). Female-centred households are marginally less food secure than male-centred households but the differences are not statistically significant. The biggest difference is with the other two household types. Nuclear and extended households are significantly more food secure (20% and 23% respectively) and significantly less severely food insecure (44% and 35%). The vulnerability of female-centred households derives from the fact that most migrant women are employed in low-paying jobs such as domestic work or as waiters in the service industry. The vulnerability of male-centred households derives from a different set of factors, primarily the difficulty of securing employment other than casual work. Both nuclear and extended households generally have two adult income earners and are therefore in a more advantageous position.

TABLE 13: Household Structure and Distribution of Food Security

Household structure	Food secure		Mildly food insecure		Moderately food insecure		Severely food insecure	
Female-centred	10	17.5	8	34.8	34	28.1	100	33.4
Male-centred	16	28.1	4	17.4	40	33.1	135	45.2
Nuclear	20	35.1	10	43.5	27	22.3	45	15.1
Extended	11	19.3	1	4.3	19	15.7	17	5.7
Total	57	100.0	23	100.0	121	100.0	299	100.0

TABLE 14: Household Structure and Levels of Food Security

Household structure	Food secure		Mildly food insecure		Moderately food insecure		Severely food insecure	
Female-centred	10	6.6	8	5.3	34	22.4	100	65.7
Male-centred	16	8.2	4	2.0	40	20.5	135	69.3
Nuclear	20	19.6	10	9.8	27	26.5	45	44.1
Extended	11	22.9	1	2.1	19	39.6	17	35.4

With regard to household size, the general principle seems to be the larger the household, the greater the chance of being food secure (Table 15). For example, only 9% of the one-person households were food secure compared with 15% of the two and three-person households and 29% of the households with four or more members. One-person households are clearly the most food insecure with 64% severely food insecure compared to around half of two and three-person households.

TABLE 15: Household Size and Levels of Food Security								
House-hold size	Food secure		Mildly food insecure		Moderately food insecure		Severely food insecure	
1	28	8.7	10	3.1	76	23.7	207	64.5
2	17	15.0	9	8.0	29	25.7	58	51.3
3	8	15.4	4	7.7	14	26.9	26	50.0
4+	4	28.6	0	0.0	2	14.3	8	57.1

Without an income, access to food in South Africa's urban areas is problematic, as virtually all foodstuffs must be purchased. As a result, food security and income are closely related. This was certainly the case with the Zimbabwean migrant households despite the fact, as noted above, that incomes were generally low. Even a small increase in monthly income has a discernible effect on food security status. As household income increases, so does the proportion of food secure households: from only 1% of households earning less than ZAR500 per month, to 11% of those earning ZAR1,501-2,000 per month, to 47% of those earning more than ZAR3,001 per month (Table 16). Similarly, the proportion of severely food insecure households declines from 89% of those earning less than ZAR500 per month to 44% of those earning ZAR1,501-2,000 per month to 28% of those earning more than ZAR3,001 per month.

TABLE 16: Household Income and Food Security				
Household income (rands per month)	Household food insecurity prevalence			
	Food secure (%)	Mildly food insecure (%)	Moderately food insecure (%)	Severely food insecure (%)
0-500	1.1	2.2	7.5	89.2
501-1,000	2.0	0.7	20.4	86.9
1,001-1,500	5.2	4.2	39.6	51.0
1,501-2,000	11.1	0.0	44.4	44.5
2,001-2,500	31.2	9.4	28.1	31.2
2,501-3,000	23.3	13.3	26.7	36.7
3,001+	47.2	17.0	7.5	28.3

The extreme vulnerability of the lowest income households was confirmed in the qualitative interviews. "You are nothing if you do not have money," is how one respondent in Cape Town described it, adding:

Here it is difficult to get anything. In Zimbabwe, we could sometimes ask people in the rural areas to send us food, but we cannot do that here. It is too far and anyway, the people in Zimbabwe will be expecting us to feed them and not vice-versa. But we are struggling here. The only days that I am okay in terms of food are on weekends because I do get paid every Friday. But by Monday or Tuesday I am back to struggling because the money is too little. My employer gives me R200 every week, but I need to pay rent and transport. It is just not enough, but there is nothing that I can do.[59]

Most confirmed that without a stable income, and given other numerous expenses, they face a massive challenge in adequately feeding themselves. Cutting back on other expenses such as rent, electricity and water charges is not an option, as eviction from their lodgings will follow. Eating less and eating cheaper foods are sometimes the only viable option.

Rising food prices are another major cause of food insecurity among urban households because of the purchasing nature of the environment. The global food price crisis that started in 2007/2008 led to a major increase in the cost of food in South Africa.[60] Although the rate of global price increases had tempered by 2011 when this survey was done, internal economic dynamics continued to cause food prices to increase much faster than average income. Only 26% of the respondents said that the household had been unaffected by rising prices in the previous year (Table 17). Around one-third had gone without food about once a month while 28% had done so once a week. The remaining 14% had this as an almost daily experience.

TABLE 17: Frequency of Going Without Food Because of Food Price Increases		
	No.	%
Never	129	25.8
About once per month	161	32.2
About once per week	142	28.4
More than once per week but less than every day of the week	40	8.0
Every day	20	4.0
Don't know	8	1.6
Total	500	100.0

In the face of food price increases, households have to revise their food budget constantly by increasing the amount of money allocated to food purchase, reducing the amount of food bought, or replacing it with cheaper alternatives when these are available. As one respondent in Johannesburg commented:

The increases are just too much. You cannot budget well in advance because of the increases. When I came to South Africa 5 years ago, things were different. You could buy a loaf of bread for the same amount of money for over a year without any changes. But now it is different. You cannot just pick a product on the shelf and take it to the till on the basis that you know the price that you bought it for the previous month. No, you can no longer do that; you have to check the price. On many occasions you see people returning or just leaving goods at the till because the price they thought the goods cost would have changed. Although the increases are better than what we experienced back home, it is still difficult because we do not have the money to make up for the increases.[61]

The foods that most households had to do without because of price increases in the previous six months included meat, poultry or offal (55% of households), cereals (53%), foods made with oil or butter (49%), and eggs (49%). In sum, over 30% of households had gone without food from all of the main food groups (Figure 11).

FIGURE 11: Types of Foods Not Consumed Because of Food Price Increases

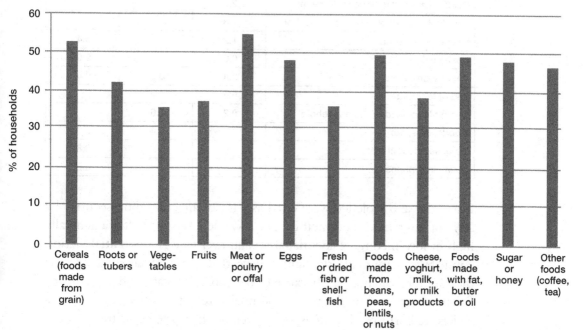

11. EXACERBATING FOOD INSECURITY

Besides rising food prices, households were asked to indicate other problems that impinged on their ability to access food and to rank them in order of importance (Table 18). Reduced income was one of the major issues affecting household food security, with 35% mentioning it as a problem and 19% as a major problem. In most cases, loss of income results from a household member losing their job, forcing the household to adjust its food intake. In Cape Town, for example, migrant workers noted that they often lose their jobs when the tourism season is off-peak and it is then that they struggle to put food on the table. Those working in the construction industry also lose their jobs in the rainy season when much construction work stops.

TABLE 18: Other Problems Impacting on Food Access			
Problem	Rank I	Rank II	Rank III
Relocation of the family	22.2	9.4	2.0
Reduced income of a household member	19.0	11.8	4.0
Theft	7.2	2.4	1.6
Accident of household member	4.2	0.4	0.2
Serious illness of household member	3.2	0.2	
Reduced remittances from relatives	2.6	3.8	3.2
Death of a working household member	2.0		
Loss/reduced employment for member	1.8		
Insecurity/violence	1.2	9.8	9.4
Health risks	0.6	0.2	2.0
Political problems	0.4	0.8	0.4
End of food aid	0.4		
Death of the head of the household	0.2	2.6	
Floods, fires, etc.		0.4	2.8
Increased cost of water			0.6
Taking in orphans			0.2

Insecurity and violence were cited as a factor affecting food security by 20% of households and theft by 11%. While levels of theft are generally high in low-income residential areas and everyone is a potential victim, Zimbabwean migrants strongly believe that they are targeted because they are foreign and that, because of their migrant status, they are insufficiently protected by the police and unable to defend themselves. These beliefs are borne out in extensive research on the xenophobic treatment of Zimbabweans in South Africa.[62] After income instability, family relocation was mentioned as the most important source of food insecurity: 34% mentioned it as a problem and 22% as the primary problem. The fact that one-third of the households had relocated in the previous six months suggests that intra and inter-urban mobility plays a role in exacerbating food insecurity. Respondents in the in-depth interviews provided additional insights into this issue, pointing out that the lack of reliable and stable accommodation was highly destabilizing to household income and therefore to food security. The difficulties of acquiring affordable accommodation often forced them to move in search of cheaper lodgings. However, funds were then needed to need to hire transport to ferry their possessions as well as pay the deposit to secure the new accommodation. One household head narrated his ordeal in trying to find cheaper alternatives for his family as follows:

> It is a difficult life when you are continuously moving. This is my second month here in Nyanga. Two months ago I had been staying in Langa, but I could no longer afford the rent, so I left. But that movement has cost me a lot of money and I am yet to fully pay the person I hired to relocate. I am lucky because I know the transporter from way back in Zimbabwe. But you know, business is business and I have to pay him. It is only that things are difficult. Now I do not know how long I will stay here. The rent was R600 for this room when I came, but I have been told that next month it will increase to R800. Now I cannot afford that amount for that is why I left Langa. Maybe I will find another cheaper place here in Nyanga where I can pay R400 or R500. What else can I do? It is difficult when you have no house.[63]

The situation described by the respondent is not untypical among migrants who try to minimize their monthly costs by seeking out cheaper accommodation, but end up incurring large and immediate costs in the relocation process.

12. Migrant Remittances and Food Security

Considerable research and policy attention has focused on the global remitting behaviour of migrants.[64] There is also a growing literature on intra-regional remitting within Southern Africa.[65] The majority of Zimbabwean migrants in South Africa left parents, sisters, brothers, children, and other relatives behind when they moved to South Africa. A number of studies have demonstrated that most Zimbabweans remit funds and goods to their families back home.[66] The respondents in this survey were no exception, periodically sending money to help with expenses like food, school fees, and clothing as well as investments in both movable and immovable assets. Most feel obligated to send money home, not least because their families are struggling to survive. One respondent in Du Noon expressed his desire to reciprocate the support he had received from his family:

> My brothers and sisters contributed money for me to come here. So I have no choice, but to look after them. They played their role, now I am playing mine. Even though it is very tough here, I have to work

hard so that they are able to live well back home. One of my brothers is still in school, so I have to pay his school fees. Maybe one day, when he finishes school he can join me here, but for now I am their only hope. So I do it, and I hope that I am making a difference in their lives. Even if I send R100 a month, I know it will help.[67]

Another saw remitting as an obligation imposed on migrants by their families:

There is a lot of pressure on some of us to send money home. It is difficult to ignore the concerns of those that are back home. Even if you do not have the money you try like a man. You can borrow from friends and work hard to return it. Sometimes the problem is that people back home think that we are making a lot of money here. So every few days you get a call and people are asking for money. It's serious...sometimes people end up not answering calls from home because you know that it is usually about money. Yes, I know they are in problems, but sometimes you need some space to make some money and stabilize. As things are, it is difficult. Maybe when the situation in Zimbabwe improves, then we can stop sending money so often.[68]

Only 18% percent of the households in this survey indicated that they were not remitting money to Zimbabwe (Table 19). Nearly 40% of remitting households sent funds to Zimbabwe at least once a month and another 41% a few times per year. Remitting is definitely a family business, with 76% sending funds to immediate family members and 27% to extended family members.

TABLE 19: Frequency of Remitting Money to Zimbabwe		
	No.	%
More than once a month	55	13.4
Once a month	107	26.2
A few times a year	166	40.7
Once a year	35	8.5
Occasionally	46	11.2
Total	409	100.0

The question of interest in this survey, and one which is rarely addressed in the literature, is what impact remitting behaviour and obligations has on the food security of migrant households in places of destination. Given that food insecurity is a significant problem among migrant households in Cape Town and Zimbabwe, to what extent is this a function of the need to remit, which reduces disposable household income and the amount available to spend on food? Alternatively, does food insecurity itself have a negative impact on remitting, affecting, for example, the amounts and frequency of remitting?

The study did find that the amounts remitted by Zimbabwean migrant households were relatively small (Figure 12). Nearly two-thirds of the remitting migrants could only remit less than ZAR500 per month, with another 18% remitting ZAR501–1,000 per month. Only 17% were sending home more than ZAR1,000 per month. Despite these small amounts, only 11% of the households indicated that remittances had a positive or very positive effect on the food security situation of the household in South Africa (Table 20). By contrast, as many as 60% said it had a negative or very negative impact on their food security. The qualitative interviews suggested that remitting forced respondents to adopt various coping strategies such as reducing the number of meals or eating smaller portions.

FIGURE 12: Amount Remitted to Zimbabwe per Month

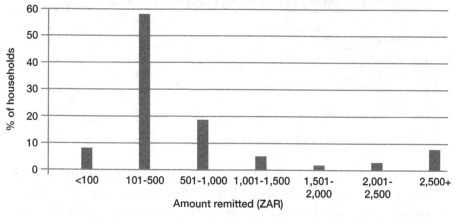

TABLE 20: Effect of Remitting Money on Migrant Household Food Security

	No.	%
Very positive	13	3.2
Positive	32	7.8
Neither positive nor negative	117	28.6
Negative	204	49.9
Very negative	43	10.5
Total	409	100.0

More than half of the surveyed migrant households were also remitting food to Zimbabwe (Table 21). Of these, 8% did so more than once a month, 27% once a month, 43% a few times a year and 11% only occasionally. Food availability in Zimbabwe was certainly greatly improved in 2011 over 2008.[69] A similar survey undertaken in 2008 would undoubtedly have found higher food flows. In AFSUN's 2008 survey of poor Harare households, 42% had received food transfers in the previous year and, of these, 43% came from other urban areas, and 20% from both rural and urban areas.[70] A follow-up survey in Harare in 2012 found that 45% had received transfers, of which 35% came from other urban areas and 25% came from both rural and urban areas.[71] In other words, while there was a slight fall in the proportion of households receiving inter-urban food transfers, a significant minority of households continued to receive food from other urban centres. Partly, this can be explained by the fact that although availability improved between 2008 and 2012, the price of food in Zimbabwe was still considerably higher than the price of similar foodstuffs in South Africa. However, respondents did say that it was expensive to carry food to Zimbabwe as buses charge per kilogram rather than on the value of the goods being taken.

TABLE 21: Frequency of Remitting Food to Zimbabwe		
	No.	%
More than once a month	21	8.5
Once a month	66	26.6
A few times a year	108	43.5
Once a year	25	10.1
Occasionally (less than once a year)	28	11.3
Total	248	100.0

Sending food to Zimbabwe definitely affected the food security situation of migrant households in South Africa. As the survey results indicate, only 13% reported the impact as positive or very positive, while 39% said the effect was negative or very negative. A greater percentage said that the impact was neither positive nor negative (48%). Only 29% said that cash remitting had neither a negative nor positive impact. Why this might be is unclear although one reason could be that those remitting food were simply sending a portion of their own food supply, while those sending money then had less to spend on food.

TABLE 22: Effect of Food Remittances on Migrant Household Food Security		
	No.	%
Very positive	16	6.5
Positive	15	6.1
Neither positive nor negative	118	48.2
Negative	78	31.9
Very negative	18	7.3
Total	245	49.0

13. CONCLUSION

This report examined the food security status of Zimbabwean migrant households in the poorer areas of two major South African cities, Johannesburg and Cape Town. The vast majority (over 80%) were food insecure in terms of the amount of food to which they had access and the quality and diversity of their diet, both of which were extremely poor. Those with higher incomes were consistently more food secure than those with low incomes. In an all-cash urban environment, with high levels of unemployment and intense job competition, and no urban agriculture, the primary determinant of food security is access to regular, paid employment. Female-centred households have access to a narrower range of employment opportunities (mostly domestic work and self-employment in the informal economy) and are more food insecure than other types of households. Overall, 40% of migrant household heads with a cash income were working in the informal economy where earnings are small and inconsistent. Another 16% were unskilled casual workers where, again, employment is unpredictable and income unreliable.

Although the measures of food insecurity used in the study are different from those in the Euro-American literature on the immigration effect and acculturation (which tend to focus more on health-related dietary outcomes), it is worth asking if these arguments have any purchase in the case of Zimbabwean migration to South Africa. Because much migration from Zimbabwe is relatively recent, insufficient time has elapsed for a systematic evaluation of the acculturation argument that diets and health tend to decline over time. Further research is certainly required on this issue. What seems clear is that Zimbabwean migrants are significantly more food insecure than other low-income households in the areas of the South African cities in which they congregate. At the same time, they are significantly less food insecure than households that have remained in Zimbabwe. This, then, both affirms and contradicts the arguments of the immigration effect. In other words, migrants are more food secure and therefore likely to be healthier than those they left behind. But, contrary to the immigration effect argument, they are worse off in terms of food access and security than local households of similar socio-economic standing.

One explanation for these differences might be that migrants do not enjoy the same employment prospects and income-generating possibilities as South Africans. Yet, rates of unemployment are generally lower among migrants than South Africans. They are certainly not high-income earners, but neither are their comparator South African households. The jobs they do hold tend to be in the lower end of the job market in the formal economy, self-employment in the informal economy, and casual and/or seasonal in nature. As a result, incomes are low and unpredictable, forcing many households to rely on more than one income stream. Migrant households have little or no access to land and resources to engage in urban agriculture and the vast majority of migrant households do not grow any of their own food. While this could be seen to put them at a significant disadvantage, rates of participation in urban agriculture are anyway generally low in Cape Town and Johannesburg.[72]

Another explanation, which seems more plausible, is the evidence that South Africa's social protection system – in particular the 14 million child grants that are dispensed every month – mitigate hunger and food insecurity among many South African households.[73] Most Zimbabwean migrant households do not have access to social grants in South Africa. On the other hand, it seems that social networks are much stronger among migrants and that informal social protection – such as food sharing and borrowing – is more common. However, these tend to be called upon at times of distress and are neither a regular nor reliable source of food. More common, particularly among the poorest and most vulnerable migrant households, is the regular use of soup kitchens run by churches, NGOs and CBOs, particularly in the inner-city areas.

Another reason for the higher levels of food insecurity among migrant households, and the fact that they are worse off than local households, appears to lie in the set of other pressures on migrant incomes. Like local households, they have to pay rent, transport costs and other daily necessities. However, a major expense incurred by migrant households that does not apply to others (unless they have strong links with family in rural areas) is remittances of cash and goods back to family in Zimbabwe. One of the primary reasons for coming to South Africa was to earn money to support those left behind. Migrants who are able to remit do so as frequently as possible. However, while this may have a positive impact on the food security of their family in Zimbabwe, it makes them a lot more vulnerable to food insecurity. As many as 60% reported that remitting of cash had a negative impact on their own food security. Fewer, but still 40%, said that remitting of foodstuffs had a similar impact.

The small literature on the impact of migrant remittances on food security tends to look only at the recipients and how their situation is improved. It does not ask the question about the impact of remitting on those who send remittances. This is largely because there is an implicit assumption that those who remit do so because they have disposable income and choose to spend it on remitting. However, the majority of Zimbabwean migrants in South Africa, struggling as they are to make ends meet, do not have much disposable income or savings on which to draw. They feel a strong obligation to remit but, in order to do so, must make choices and compromises because of their limited and unpredictable income. Food, though a necessity, is one of the first things to be sacrificed. Quantities decline, fewer meals are eaten, cheaper foods are preferred, and dietary quality and diversity inevitably suffer.

While migrants were generally dissatisfied with the shrinking job market in South Africa, as well as poor remuneration and the resultant negative impact on their household's food security, return to Zimbabwe was not viewed with any enthusiasm. Around 23% of those interviewed in the survey said that their household food security situation would improve if they returned. However, more than twice as many (54%) said that the impact would be negative or very negative. Most argued that the economic situation in Zimbabwe had not stabilized sufficiently to warrant return and that the likelihood of finding a job on return was low. As a result, the household's food security situation would worsen. In other words, while food insecurity in Zimbabwe is a major driver of migration to South Africa, food insecurity in South Africa is unlikely to encourage many to return.

ENDNOTES

1   J. Crush and D. Tevera (eds) *Zimbabwe's Exodus: Crisis, Migration, Survival* (Cape Town and Ottawa: SAMP and IDRC, 2010); J. Crush, A. Chikanda and G. Tawodzera, *The Third Wave: Mixed Migration from Zimbabwe to South Africa*. SAMP Migration Policy Series No. 59, Cape Town, 2012.

2   Crush and Tevera, *Zimbabwe's Exodus;* J. McGregor and R. Primorac, *Zimbabwe's New Diaspora: Displacement and the Cultural Politics of Survival* (Berghahn Books, 2010: B. Derman and R. Kaarhus (eds), *In the Shadow of a Conflict: Crisis in Zimbabwe and Its Effects in Mozambique, South Africa and Zambia* (Harare: Weaver Press, 2013).

3   S. Johnston, A. Bernstein, and R. de Villiers (eds) *Migration from Zimbabwe: Numbers, Needs, and Policy Options* (Johannesburg: Centre for Development and Enterprise, 2008); D. Makina, "Zimbabwe in Johannesburg" In Crush and Tevera, *Zimbabwe's Exodus*, pp. 225-41; Crush et al., *The Third Wave.*

4   A. Bloch, "The Right to Rights? Undocumented Migrants from Zimbabwe Living in South Africa" *Sociology* 44(2) (2010): 233–50; S. Morreira, "Seeking Solidarity: Zimbabwean Undocumented Migrants in Cape Town" *Journal of Southern African Studies* 36(2) (2010): 433-48; B. Rutherford, "The Uneasy Ties of Working and Belonging: The Changing Situation for Undocumented Zimbabwean Migrants in Northern South Africa" *Ethnic and Racial Studies* 34(8) (2011): 1303-19. S. Morreira, "'You Can't Just Step From One Place to Another':

The Socio-Politics of Illegality in Migration from Zimbabwe to South Africa" *Migration Letters* 12 (2015).

5   A. Chikanda, "Skilled Health Professionals' Migration and Its Impact on Health Delivery in Zimbabwe" *Journal of Ethnic and Migration Studies* 32(4) (2007): 667-80; A. Chikanda, "Medical Migration from Zimbabwe in the post-ESAP Era: Magnitude, Causes and Impact on the Poor" *Development Southern Africa* 24(1) (2007): 47-60; A. Chikanda, "The Migration of Health Professionals from Zimbabwe" In J. Connell (ed) *The International Migration of Health Workers,* (New York and London: Routledge, 2008), pp. 110-28; A. Chikanda, "Nursing the Health System: The Migration of Health Professionals from Zimbabwe" In Crush and Tevera, *Zimbabwe's Exodus,* pp. 133-52. D. Ranga, "The Role of Politics in the Migration of Zimbabwean Teachers to South Africa" *Development Southern Africa* 32(2015): 258-73.

6   A. Chikanda, *The Engagement of the Zimbabwean Medical Diaspora,* SAMP Policy Series No. 55, Cape Town, 2011; J. McGregor and D. Pasura, "Diasporic Repositioning and the Politics of Re-engagement: Developmentalising Zimbabwe's Diaspora" *Round Table* 99 (2010): 687-703.

7   D. Makina, "Determinants of Return Migration Intentions: Evidence from Zimbabwean Migrants Living in South Africa" *Development Southern Africa* 29(2012): 365-78.

8   Human Rights Watch, "Keep Your Head Down: Unprotected Migrants in South Africa" *Human Rights Watch* 19(3) (2007): 1-11; E. Worby, "Address Unknown: The Temporality of Displacement and the Ethics of Disconnection among Zimbabwean Migrants in Johannesburg" *Journal of Southern African Studies* 36(2) (2010): 417-31; K. Lefko-Everett, "The Voices of Migrant Zimbabwean Women in South Africa" In Crush and Tevera, *Zimbabwe's Exodus,* pp. 269-87; A. Mawadza, "The Nexus Between Migration and Human Security: Zimbabwean Migrants in South Africa" Paper No 162, Institute for Security Studies, Pretoria, 2011; B. Rutherford, "The Politics of Boundaries: The Shifting Terrain of Belonging in a South African Border Zone" *African Diaspora* 4(2) (2011): 207-29; J. Crush and G. Tawodzera, "Medical Xenophobia and Zimbabwean Migrant Access to Public Health Services in South Africa" *Journal of Ethnic and Migration Studies* 40: 655-70.

9   M. Bolt, "Camaraderie and its Discontents: Class Consciousness, Ethnicity and Divergent Masculinities among Zimbabwean Migrant Farmworkers in South Africa" *Journal of Southern African Studies* 36(2) (2010); N. Matshaka, "'Marobot neMawaya': Traffic Lights and Wire: Crafting Zimbabwean Migrant Masculinities in Cape Town" *Feminist Africa* 13 (2009): 65-86; O. Sibanda, "Social Ties and the Dynamics of Integration in the City of Johannesburg among Zimbabwe Migrants" *Journal of Sociology and Social Anthropology* 1(1-2) (2010): 47-57; J. Muzondidya, "Makwerekwere: Migration, Citizenship and Identity among Zimbabweans in South Africa" In McGregor and Primorac, *Zimbabwe's New Diaspora,* pp. 37-58; C. Hungwe, "The Uses of Social Capital Among Zimbabwean Migrants in Johannesburg" *Africa Review* 7(2015): 121-33; P. Mangezvo, "Xenophobic Exclusion and Masculinities among Zimbabwean Male Migrants: The Case of Cape Town and Stellenbosch" DPhil Thesis, Stellenbosch University, 2015.

10   B. Rutherford and L. Addison, "Zimbabwean Farm Workers in Northern South Africa: Transnational Strategies of Survival in an Ambivalent Border-Zone" *Review of African Political Economy* 34 (2007): 619-35; E. Sisulu, B. Moyo and

N. Tshuma, "The Zimbabwean Community in South Africa" In R. Southall, S. Buhlungu, J. Daniel and J Lutchman (eds) *State of the Nation: South Africa,* (Cape Town: HSRC, 2007), pp. 552-75; S. Mosala, "The Work Experience of Zimbabwean Migrants in South Africa" Issue Paper No. 33, ILO Sub-Regional Office for Southern Africa, Harare, 2008; L. Moorhouse and P. Cunningham, "Permanently 'In Process': The Intersection of Migration, Work Identity and the Reality of Human Resource Development in the South African Context" *Human Resource Development International* 13(5) (2010): 587-97; B. Rutherford, "Zimbabweans on the Farms of Northern South Africa" In Crush and Tevera, *Zimbabwe's Exodus,* pp. 244-65; E. Idemudia, J. Williams and G. Wyatt, "Migration Challenges Among Zimbabwean Refugees Before, During and Post Arrival in South Africa" *Journal of Injury and Violence Research* 5(1) (2011): 21. P. Blaauw, A. Pretorius, C. Schoeman and R. Schenck, "Explaining Migrant Wages: The Case Of Zimbabwean Day Labourers In South Africa" *International Business & Economics Research Journal* (11) (2012); M. Bolt, "Producing Permanence: Employment, Domesticity and the Flexible Future on a South African Border Farm" *Economy and Society* 42(2013): 197-225; L. Addison, "Delegated Despotism: Frontiers of Agrarian Labour on a South African Border Farm" *Journal of Agrarian Change* 14(2014): 286-304.

11   A. Bloch, "Emigration from Zimbabwe: Migrant Perspectives" *Social Policy & Administration* 40(1) (2006): 67-87; C. Baumann, "A Legal and Ethical Analysis of the South African Government's Response Towards Zimbabwean Immigrants" M.A. Thesis, Stellenbosch University, 2010; N. Kriger, "The Politics of Legal Status for Zimbabweans in South Africa" In McGregor and Primorac, *Zimbabwe's New Diaspora,* pp. 77-100; T. Polzer, "Silence and Fragmentation: South African Responses to Zimbabwean Migration" In Crush and Tevera, *Zimbabwe's Exodus,* pp. 363-76. A. Hammerstad, "Securitisation from Below: The Relationship between Immigration and Foreign Policy in South Africa's Approach to the Zimbabwe Crisis" *Conflict, Security & Development* 12(2012): 1-30.

12   J. Crush, "Linking Food Security, Migration and Development" *International Migration* 51(2013): 61-75.

13   T. Lacroix, "Migration, Rural Development, Poverty and Food Security: A Comparative Perspective" Report for Commonwealth Secretariat, International Migration Institute, Oxford, 2011.

14   D. Ratha, S. Mohapatra, C. Özden, S. Plaza, W. Shaw and A. Shimeles, *Leveraging Migration for Africa: Remittances, Skills, and Investment* (Washington DC: World Bank, 2011).

15   Ibid., p. 64.

16   J. Crush and W. Pendleton, "Remitting for Survival: Rethinking the Development Potential of Remittances in Southern Africa" *Global Development Studies* 5(2009): 1-28.

17   J-I. Anton, "The Impact of Remittances on Nutritional Status of Children in Ecuador" *International Migration Review* 44(2010): 269-99; A. Zezza, C. Carletto, B. Davis and P. Winters, "Assessing the Impact of Migration on Food and Nutrition Security" *Food Policy* 36 (2011): 1-6; H. Gartaula, A. Niehof and L. Visser, "Shifting Perceptions of Food Security and Land in the Context of Labour Out-Migration in Rural Nepal" *Food Security* 4(2012): 181-94; H. Sharma, "Migration, Remittance and Food Security: A Complex Relationship" *Development Review* 1(2012): 40-63; P. Samaratunga, R. Jayaweera and N. Perera,

"Impact of Migration and Remittances on Investment in Agriculture and Food Security in Sri Lanka" Agricultural Economic Policy Series No.8, Institute of Policy Studies of Sri Lanka, 2012; E. Graham and L. Gordan, "Does Having a Migrant Parent Reduce the Risk of Undernutrition for Children Who Stay behind in South-East Asia?" *Asian and Pacific Migration Journal* 22 (2013): 315-47.

18   R. Babatunde and M. Qaim, "Impact of Off-Farm Income on Food Security and Nutrition in Nigeria" *Food Policy* 35(2010): 303-11; R. Generoso, "How do Rainfall Variability, Food Security and Remittances Interact? The Case of Rural Mali" *Ecological Economics* 114(2015): 188-98.

19   Lacroix, "Migration, Rural Development, Poverty and Food Security" p. 34.

20   Crush and Pendleton, "Remitting for Survival."

21   E. Karamba, E. Quiñones and P. Winters, "Migration and Food Consumption Patterns in Ghana" *Food Policy* 36(2011): 41-53.

22   K. Fennelly, "The Healthy Migrant Phenomenon" In P. Walker and E. Day, eds., *Immigrant Medicine: A Comprehensive Reference for the Care of Refugees and Immigrants* (New York: Elsevier, 2007), pp. 612-25; L. Rubalcava, G. Teruel, D. Thomas and N. Goldman, "The Healthy Migrant Effect: New Findings From the Mexican Family Life Survey" *American Journal of Public Health* 98(2008): 78-84; J. Dean and K. Wilson, "My Health Has Improved Because I Always Have Everything I Need Here…: A Qualitative Exploration of Health Improvement and Decline Among Immigrants" *Social Science & Medicine* 70(2010): 1219-28. A. Nolan, "The 'Healthy Immigrant' Effect: Initial Evidence for Ireland" *Health Economics, Policy and Law* 7(2012): 343-62; A. Girard and P. Sercia, "Immigration and Food Insecurity: Social and Nutritional Issues for Recent Immigrants in Montreal, Canada" *International Journal of Migration, Health and Social Care* 9 (2013): 32-45.

23   S. Kennedy, J. McDonald and N. Biddle, "The Healthy Immigrant Effect and Immigrant Selection: Evidence from Four Countries" at http://carleton.ca/sppa/wp-content/uploads/chesg-mcdonald.pdf

24   C. Hadley, A. Zodhiates and D. Sellen, "Acculturation, Economics and Food Insecurity Among Refugees Resettled in the USA: A Case Study of West African Refugees" *Public Health and Nutrition* 10(2007): 405-12; J. Dharod, J. Croom and C. Sady, "Food Insecurity: Its Relationship to Dietary Intake and Body Weight among Somali Refugee Women in the United States" *Journal of Nutrition Education and Behavior* 45(2013): 47-53.

25   G. Ayala, B. Baquero and S. Klinger, "A Systematic Review of the Relationship between Acculturation and Diet among Latinos in the United States: Implications for Future Research" *Journal of the American Dietetic Association* 108(2008): 1330-44; J. Dharod, J. Croom, C. Sady and D. Morrell, "Dietary Intake, Food Security, and Acculturation Among Somali Refugees in the United States: Results of a Pilot Study" *Journal of Immigrant & Refugee Studies* 9(2011): 82-97; G. Holmboe-Ottesen and M. Wandel, "Changes in Dietary Habits after Migration and Consequences for Health: A Focus on South Asians in Europe" *Food & Nutrition Research* (2012); A. Martinez, "Reconsidering Acculturation in Dietary Change Research Among Latino Immigrants: Challenging the Preconditions of US Migration" *Ethnicity & Health* 18(2013): 115-35; I. Lesser, D. Gasevic and S. Lear, "The Association Between Acculturation and Dietary Patterns of South Asian Immigrants" *PLoS One* 18(2014): e88495; D. Sanou, E. O'Reilly, I. Ngnie-Teta, M. Batal, N. Mondain, C. Andrew, B. Newbold and I. Bourgeault, "Acculturation and Nutritional Health of Immigrants in Canada: A Scoping Review" *Journal of*

Immigrant and Minority Health 16(2014): 24–34; M. Tseng, D. Wright and C. Fang, "Acculturation and Dietary Change Among Chinese Immigrant Women in the United States" *Journal of Immigrant and Minority Health* 17 (2015): 400-7.

26   F. Perez-Cueto, W. Verbeke, C. Lachat, A. Remaut-De Winter, "Changes in Dietary Habits Following Temporal Migration: The Case of International Students in Belgium" *Appetite* 52 (2009): 83–8; M. Guendelman, S. Cheryan and B. Monin, "Fitting In But Getting Fat: Identity Threat and Dietary Choices Among U.S. Immigrant Groups" *Psychological Science* 22(2011): 959-67; P. Guarnaccia, T. Vivar, A. Bellows and G. Alcaraz, "'We Eat Meat Every Day': Ecology and Economy of Dietary Change Among Oaxacan Migrants from Mexico to New Jersey" *Ethnic and Racial Studies* 35(2012): 104-19; L. Vera-Becerra, M. Lopez and L. Kaiser, "Child Feeding Practices and Overweight Status Among Mexican Immigrant Families" *Journal of Immigrant and Minority Health* 17(2015): 375-82; H-H. Nguyen, C. Smith, G. Reynolds and B. Freshman, "The Effect of Acculturation on Obesity Among Foreign-Born Asians Residing in the United States" *Journal of Immigrant and Minority Health* 17(2015): 389-99; C. Oh and E. Saito, "Comparison of Eating Habits in Obese and Non-obese Filipinas Living in an Urban Area of Japan" *Journal of Immigrant and Minority Health* 17 (2015): 467-73; H-H. Nguyen, C. Smith, G. Reynolds and B. Freshman, "The Effect of Acculturation on Obesity Among Foreign-Born Asians Residing in the United States" *Journal of Immigrant and Minority Health* 17(2015): 389-99.

27   F. Perez-Cueto, W. Verbeke, C. Lachat, A. Remaut-De Winter, "Changes in Dietary Habits Following Temporal Migration: The Case of International Students in Belgium" *Appetite* 52 (2009): 83–8.

28   A. Renzaho and C. Burns, "Post-Migration Food Habits of Sub-Saharan African Migrants in Victoria: A Cross-Sectional Study" *Nutrition & Dietetics* 63(2006): 91-102; C. Méjean, P. Traissac, S. Eymard-Duvernay, J. El Ati, F. Delpeuch and B. Maire, "Diet Quality of North African Migrants in France Partly Explains their Lower Prevalence of Diet-Related Chronic Conditions Relative to their Native Peers" *Journal of Nutrition* 137(2007): 2106-13; H. Delisle, J. Vioque and A. Gil, "Dietary Patterns and Quality in West-African Immigrants in Madrid" *Nutrition Journal* 8(2009); H. Venters and F. Gany, "African Immigrant Health" *Journal of Immigrant and Minority Health* 13(2011): 333-44; A. Gele and A. Mbalilaki, "Overweight and Obesity among African Immigrants in Oslo" *BMC Research Notes* 6:119 (2013); M-T. Okafor, O. Carter-Pokras and M.Zhan, "Greater Dietary Acculturation (Dietary Change) Is Associated With Poorer Current Self-Rated Health Among African Immigrant Adults" *Journal of Nutrition Education and Behavior* 46(2014): 226-35.

29   Crush et al., *The Third Wave.*

30   Crush and Tevera, *Zimbabwe's Exodus.*

31   D. Tevera and A. Chikanda, "Development Impact of International Remittances: Some Evidence from Origin Households in Zimbabwe" *Global Development Studies* 5(2009): 273-302.

32   Crush et al., *The Third Wave.*

33   Ibid.

34   Makina, "Zimbabwe in Johannesburg"; Hungwe, "Uses of Social Capital Among Zimbabwean Migrants in Johannesburg"; Mangezvo, "Xenophobic Exclusion and Masculinities among Zimbabwean Male Migrants."

35   Crush et al., *The Third Wave.*

36   B. Dodson, "Gender, Migration and Livelihoods: Migrant Women in Southern Africa" In N. Piper (ed.), *New Perspectives on Gender and Migration: Livelihood, Rights and Entitlements* (London: Routledge, 2013), pp. 137-58.

37   Ibid.

38   Derman and Kaarhus, *In the Shadow of a Conflict.*

39   G. Tawodzera, J. Crush and L. Zanamwe, *The State of Food Insecurity in Harare, Zimbabwe,* African Food Security Urban Network (AFSUN), Cape Town, 2012.

40   Makina, "Zimbabwe in Johannesburg."

41   R. Amit, "The Zimbabwean Documentation Process: Lessons Learned" ACMS Research Report, University of the Witwatersrand, Johannesburg, 2011.

42   Crush et al., *The Third Wave,* p. 26.

43   R. Mattes, M. Bratton and Y. Davids, "Poverty, Survival and Democracy in Southern Africa" Afrobarometer, Working Paper Number 23, Cape Town, 2003; Afrobarometer, "Poverty, Poverty Measurement and Democracy in Southern Africa" Afrobarometer Briefing Paper Number 4, Cape Town, 2003.

44   J. Coates, A. Swindale and P. Bilinsky, "Household Food Insecurity Access Scale (HFIAS) for Measurement of Food Access: Indicator Guide (Version 3)" Food and Nutrition Technical Assistance Project, Academy for Educational Development, Washington DC, 2007.

45   Ibid.

46   A. Swindale and P. Bilinsky, "Household Dietary Diversity Score (HDDS) for Measurement of Household Food Access: Indicator Guide (Version 2)" Food and Nutrition Technical Assistance Project, Academy for Educational Development, Washington DC, 2006.

47   P. Bilinsky and A. Swindale, "Months of Adequate Household Food Provisioning (MAHFP) for Measurement of Household Food Access: Indicator Guide" Food and Nutrition Technical Assistance Project, Academy for Educational Development, Washington DC, 2007.

48   J. Battersby, *The State of Urban Food Insecurity in Cape Town,* AFSUN Urban Food Security Series No. 11, Cape Town, 2011; M. Rudolph, F. Kroll, S. Ruysenaar and T. Dlamini, *The State of Food Insecurity in Johannesburg,* AFSUN Urban Food Security Series No. 12, Cape Town, 2012.

49   Interview No. 9, Central Johannesburg, 12 November 2011.

50   Interview No. 2, Johannesburg, 11 November 2011.

51   Interview No. 19, Johannesburg, 16 November 2011.

52   Interview No. 26, Du Noon, Cape Town, 25 November 2011.

53   J. Crush and B. Frayne, "Supermarket Expansion and the Informal Food Economy in Southern African Cities: Implications for Urban Food Security" *Journal of Southern African Studies* 37(2011): 781-807; S. Peyton, W. Moseley and J. Battersby, "Implications of Supermarket Expansion on Urban Food Security in Cape Town, South Africa" *African Geographical Review* 34(2015): 36-54.

54   Interview No. 28, Du Noon, Cape Town, 25 November 2011.

55   Hungwe, "Uses of Social Capital Among Zimbabwean Migrants in Johannesburg."

56   NGOs and churches are able to access food for redistribution through the

Johannesburg food bank; see D. Warshawsky, *Urban Food Insecurity and the Advent of Food Banking in Southern Africa,* AFSUN Urban Food Security Series No. 6, Cape Town, 2010.

57 Participant in Focus Group Discussion, Johannesburg Central, 13th November 2011. Studies of the role of the Central Methodist Church in assisting migrants and refugees in inner-city Johannesburg include B. Bompani, "Local Religious Organisations Performing Development: Refugees in the Central Methodist Mission in Johannesburg" *Journal of International Development* (published online, 2013) and C. Kuljiab, Sanctuary: *How an Inner-city Church Spilled onto a Sidewalk* (Johannesburg: Jacana, 2013).

58 Interview No. 48, Masiphumelele, Cape Town, 1 December 2011.

59 Interview No. 36, Nyanga, Cape Town, 28 November 2011.

60 T. Jayne, A. Chapoto, I. Minde and C. Donovan, "The 2008/09 Food Price and Food Security Situation in Eastern and Southern Africa" MSU International Development Working Paper No. 97, Michigan State University, East Lansing, 2008; G. Rapsomaniikis, "The 2007-2008 Food Price Episode: Impact and Policies in Eastern and Southern Africa" FAO Commodities and Trade Technical Paper No. 12, Rome, 2009.

61 Interview Number 12, Alexandra Park, Johannesburg, 14 November 2011.

62 See Endnote No. 8.

63 Interview Number 38, Nyanga, Cape Town, 28 November 2011.

64 S. Maimbo and D. Ratha (eds.). *Remittances: Development Impact and Future Prospects* (Washington DC: World Bank, 2005); R. Adams Jnr., "Evaluating the Economic Impact of International Remittances on Developing Countries using Household Surveys: A Literature Review" *Journal of Development Studies* 47(2011): 809-28; D. Ratha, S. Mohapatra, C. Özden, S. Plaza, W. Shaw and A. Shimeles, eds., *Leveraging Migration for Africa: Remittances, Skills, and Investments* (Washington DC: World Bank, 2011); T. van Naerssen, L. Smith, T. Davids and M. Marchand (eds.), *Women, Gender, Remittances and Development in the Global South* (Farnham: Ashgate: 2015).

65 B. Dodson, *Gender, Migration and Remittances in Southern Africa,* SAMP Migration Policy Series No. 49, Cape Town, 2008; Crush and Pendleton, "Remitting for Survival: Rethinking the Development Potential of Remittances in Southern Africa"; B. Frayne and W. Pendleton, "The Development Role of Remittances in the Urbanization Process in Southern Africa" *Global Development Studies* 5(2008/9): 85-132; FinMark Trust, "SADC Remittance Flows Report" Johannesburg, 2011.

66 F. Maphosa, "Remittances and Development: The Impact of Migration to South Africa on Rural Livelihoods in Southern Zimbabwe" *Development Southern Africa* 24(1) (2007): 123-36; S. Kerzner, "'Cash and Carry': Understanding the Johannesburg-Zimbabwe Remittance Corridor" Report for FinMark Trust, Johannesburg, 2009; S. Bracking and L. Sachikonye, "Migrant Remittances and Household Wellbeing in Urban Zimbabwe" *International Migration* 48(5) (2010): 203–27; D. Von Burgsdorff, "The South Africa-Zimbabwe Remittance Corridor: An Analysis of Key Drivers and Constraints" MCom Thesis, University of Cape Town, 2010; T. Mukwedeva, "Zimbabwe's Saving Grace: The Role of Remittances in Household Livelihood Strategies in Glen Norah, Harare" *South African Review of Sociology* 42(1) (2011): 116-30; V. Thebe, "From South

Africa With Love: The *Mayalisha* System and Households' Quest for Livelihood Reconstruction in South-Western Zimbabwe" *Journal of Modern African Studies* 49 (2011): 647-70; D. von Burgsdorff, "Strangling the Lifeline: An Analysis of Remittance Flows from South Africa to Zimbabwe," Report for PASSOP, Cape Town, 2012; D. Makina, "Financial Access for Migrants and Intermediation of Remittances in South Africa" *International Migration* 51(2013): e133–e147; D. Makina, "Migration and Characteristics of Remittance Senders in South Africa" *International Migration* 51(2013): e148-e158.

67   Interview No. 35, Du Noon, Cape Town, 26 November 2011.

68   Participant in Focus Group Discussion, Masiphumelele, Cape Town, 1 December 2011.

69   G. Tawodzera, "Household Food Insecurity and Survival in Harare: 2008 and Beyond" *Urban Forum* 25(2014): 207-16.

70   Tawodzera et al. *State of Food Insecurity in Harare.*

71   Tawodzera, "Household Food Insecurity and Survival in Harare."

72   J. Crush, A. Hovorka and D. Tevera, "Food Security in Southern African Cities: The Place of Urban Agriculture" *Progress in Development Studies* 11(4): 285-305.

73   L. Patel, "Poverty, Gender and Social Protection: Child Support Grants in Soweto, South Africa" *Journal of Policy Practice* 11 (2012): 106-20; L. Patel and T. Hochfeld, "It Buys Food but Does it Change Gender Relations? Child Support Grants in Soweto, South Africa" *Gender & Development* 19(2011): 229-40.

Printed in the United States
By Bookmasters